The Adventures of Strawberryhead & Gingerbread™

The Barking Lot Series ⑥

Cursive Writing Alphabet Soup Workbook

The
Adventures of
Strawberryhead
& Gingerbread™

The Barking Lot Series ⑥
Cursive Writing Alphabet
Soup Workbook

KF Wheatie & KM Wheatie

Strawberryhead &
Gingerbread Press

www.strawberryheadandgingerbread.com

The Adventures of Strawberryhead & Gingerbread™,
The Barking Lot Series ⑥ Cursive Writing Alphabet Soup Workbook

Published by Strawberryhead and Gingerbread Press
https://www.strawberryheadandgingerbread.com

ISBN: 979-8-9900656-1-1

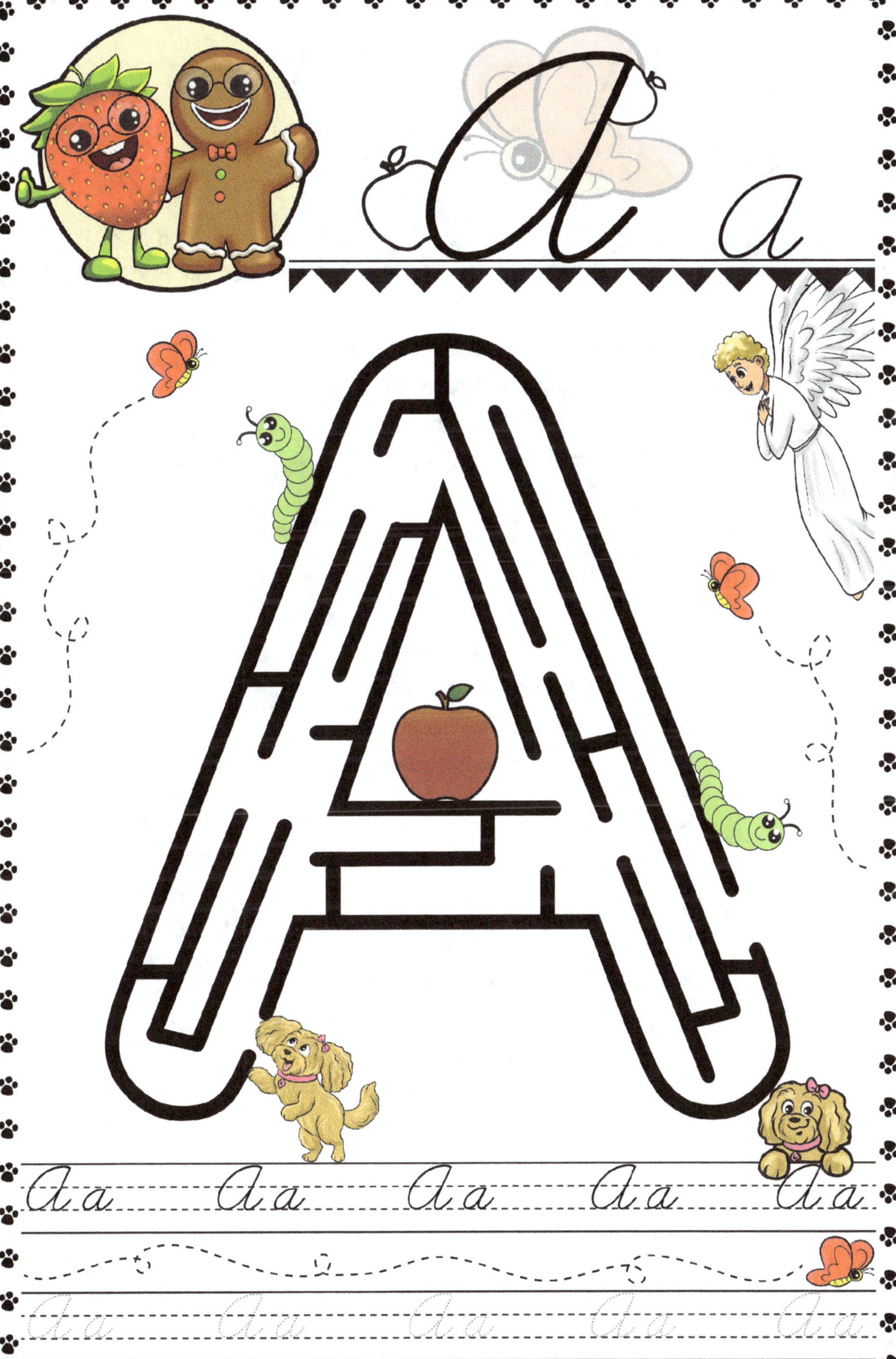

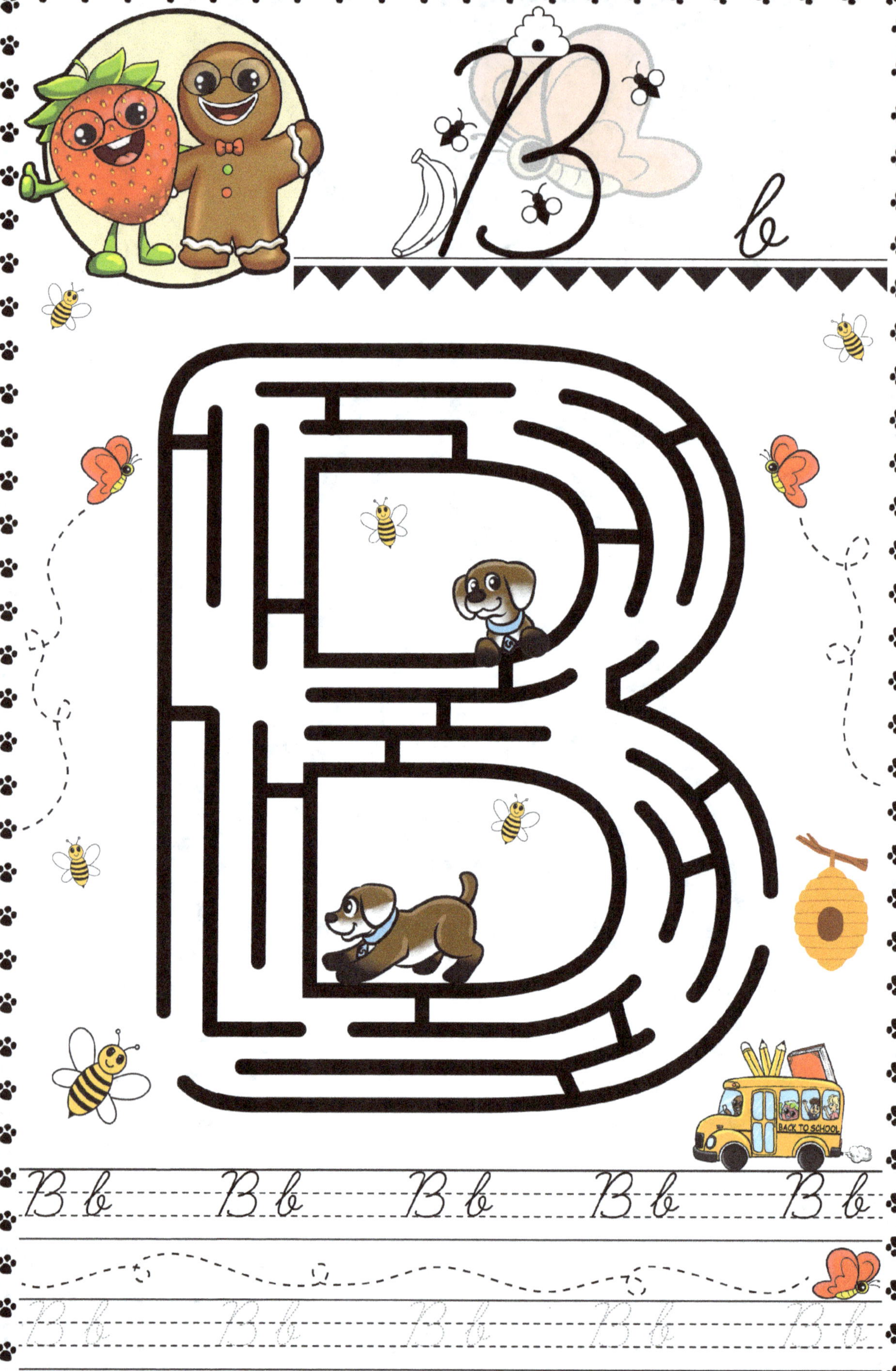

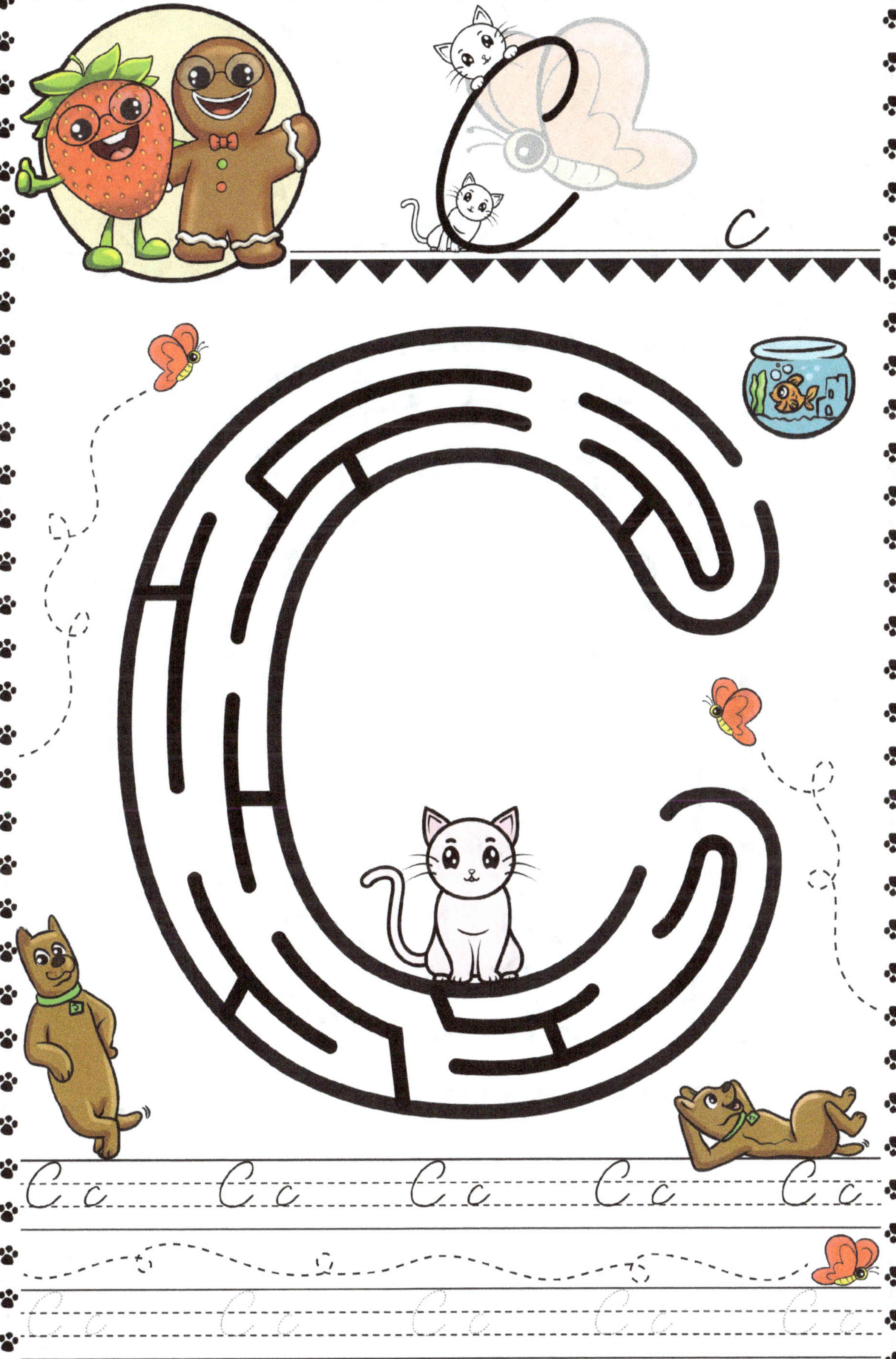

c
Cc Cc Cc Cc Cc

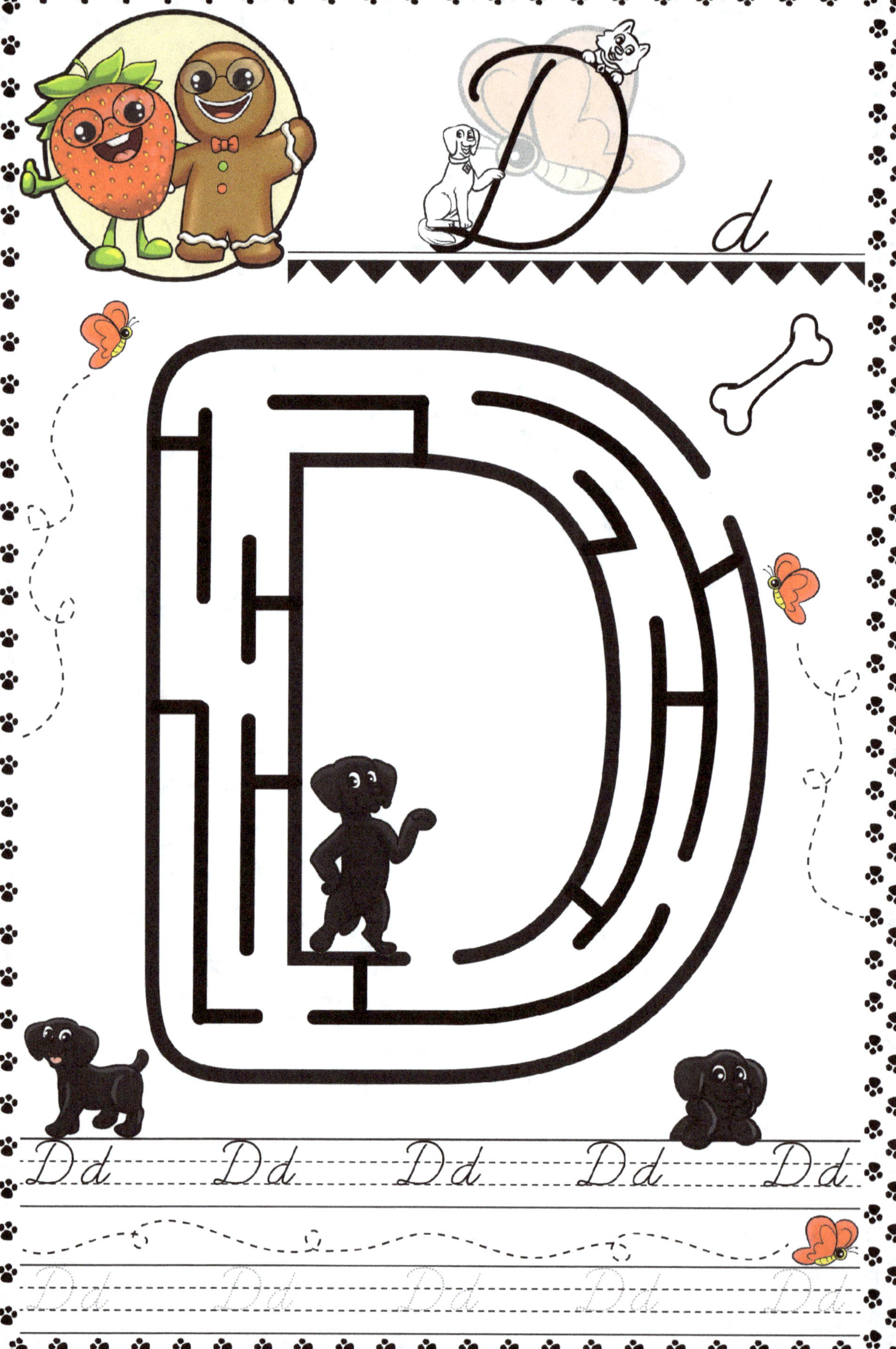

Dd Dd Dd Dd Dd

Dd Dd Dd Dd Dd

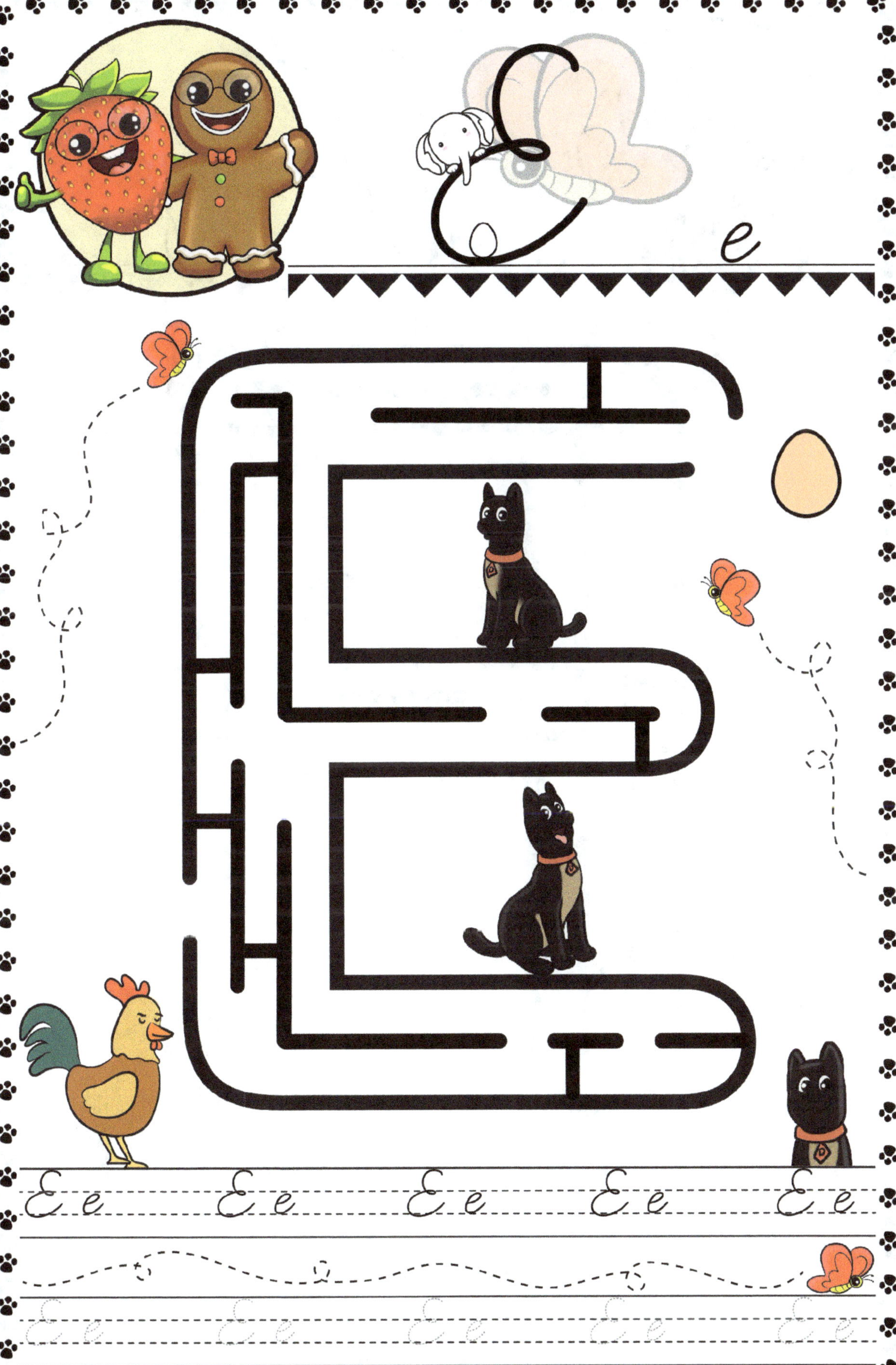
e
Ee   Ee   Ee   Ee   Ee

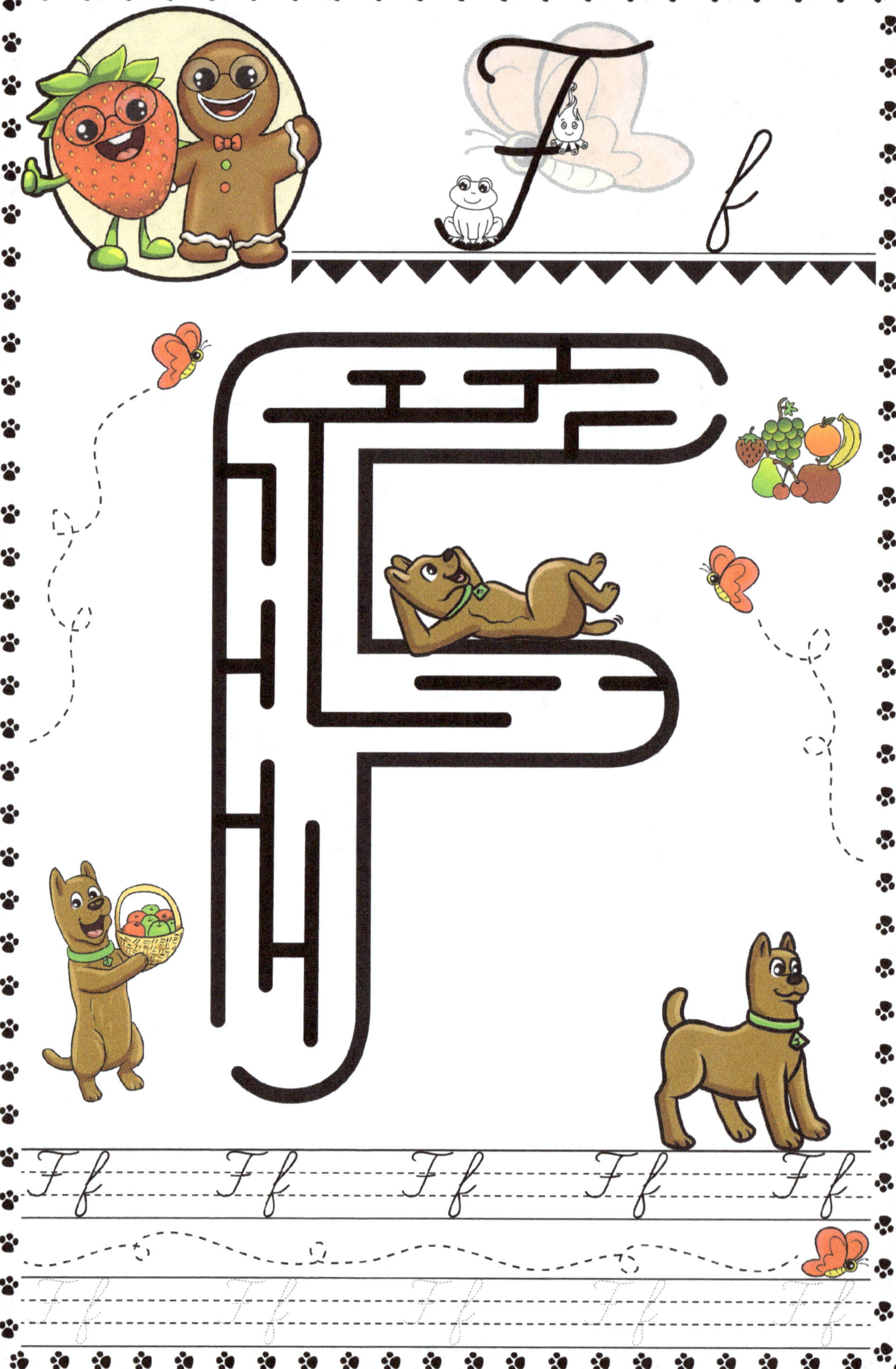

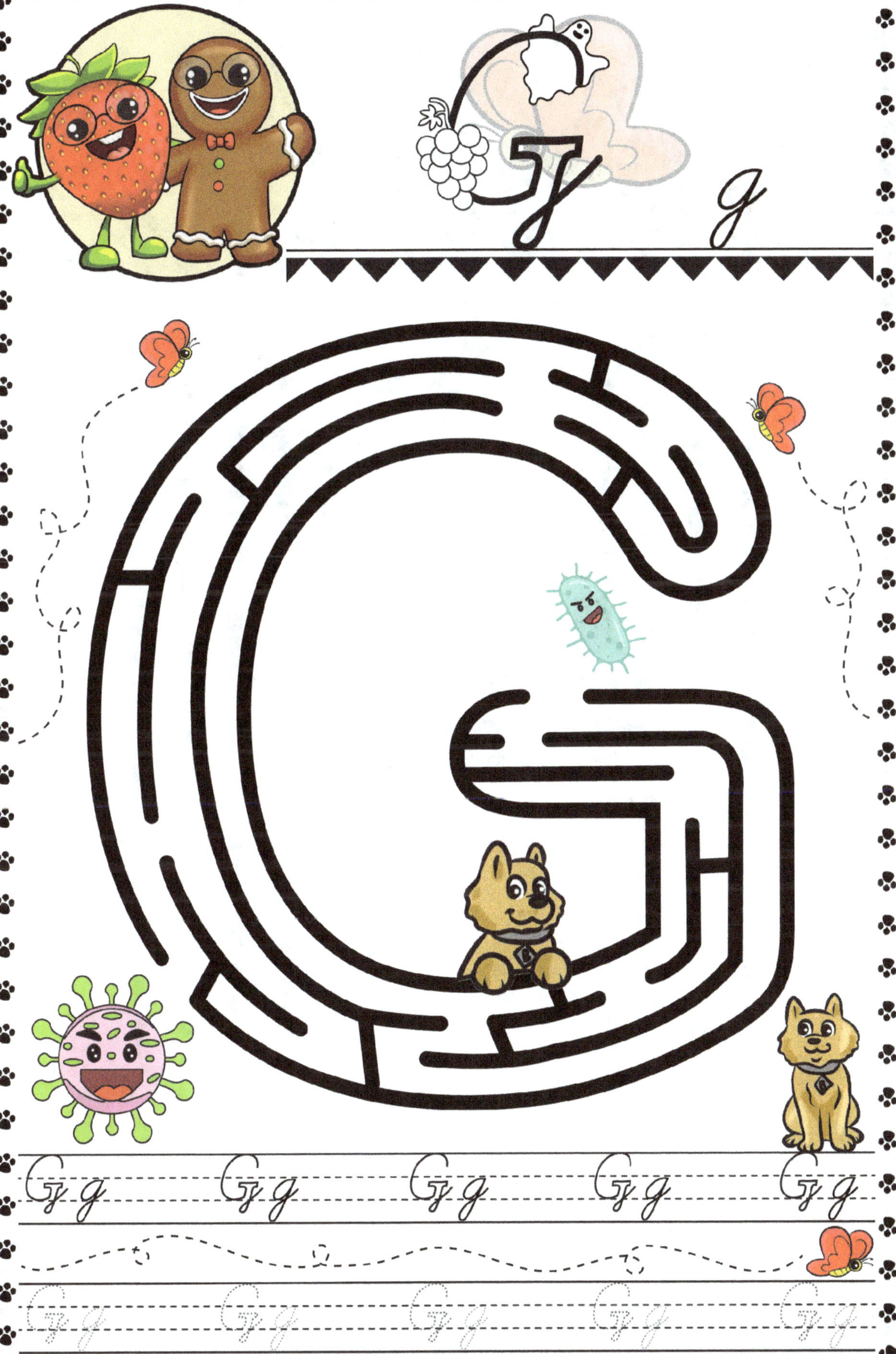

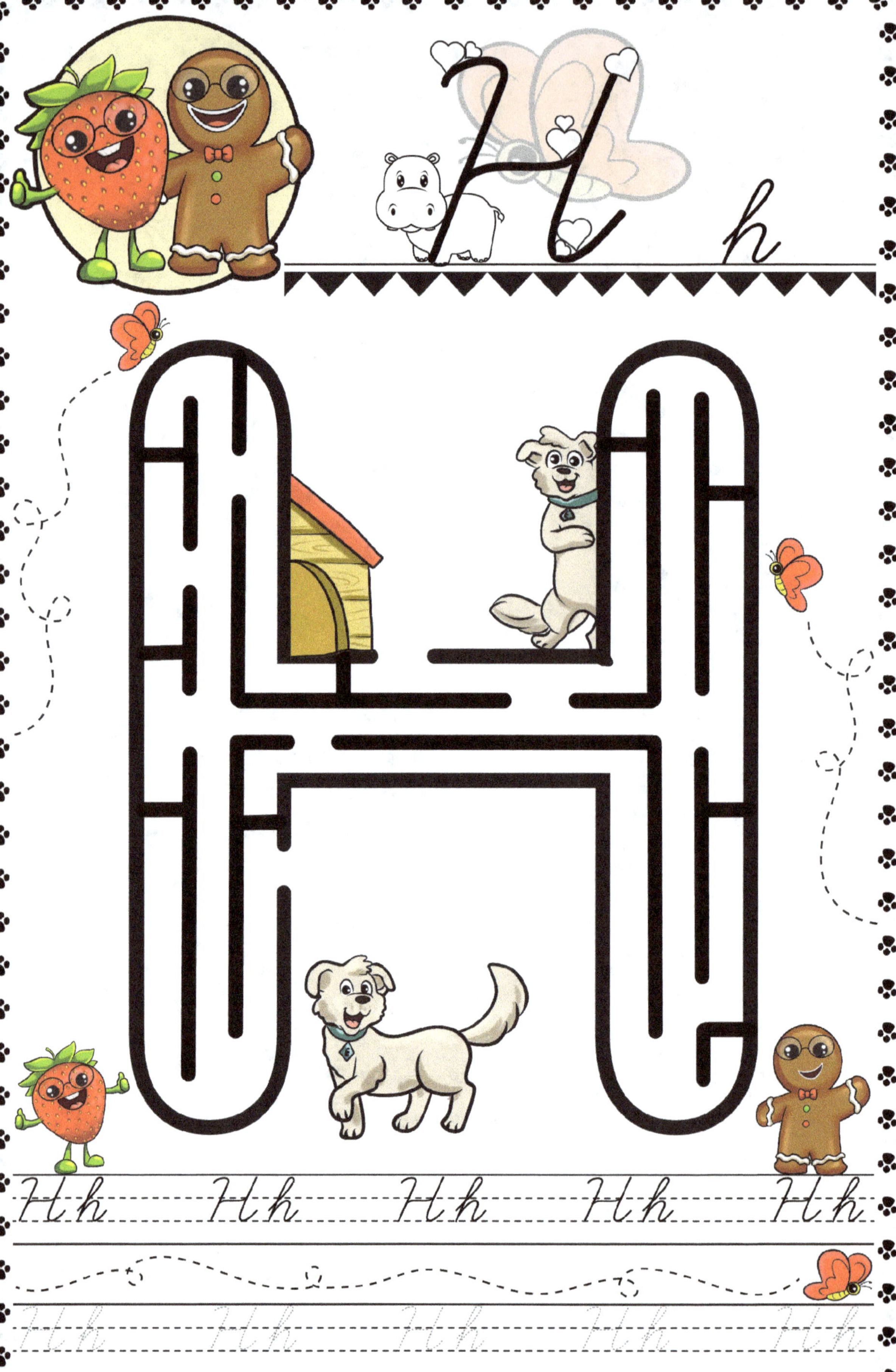

H h
Hh   Hh   Hh   Hh   Hh
Hh   Hh   Hh   Hh   Hh

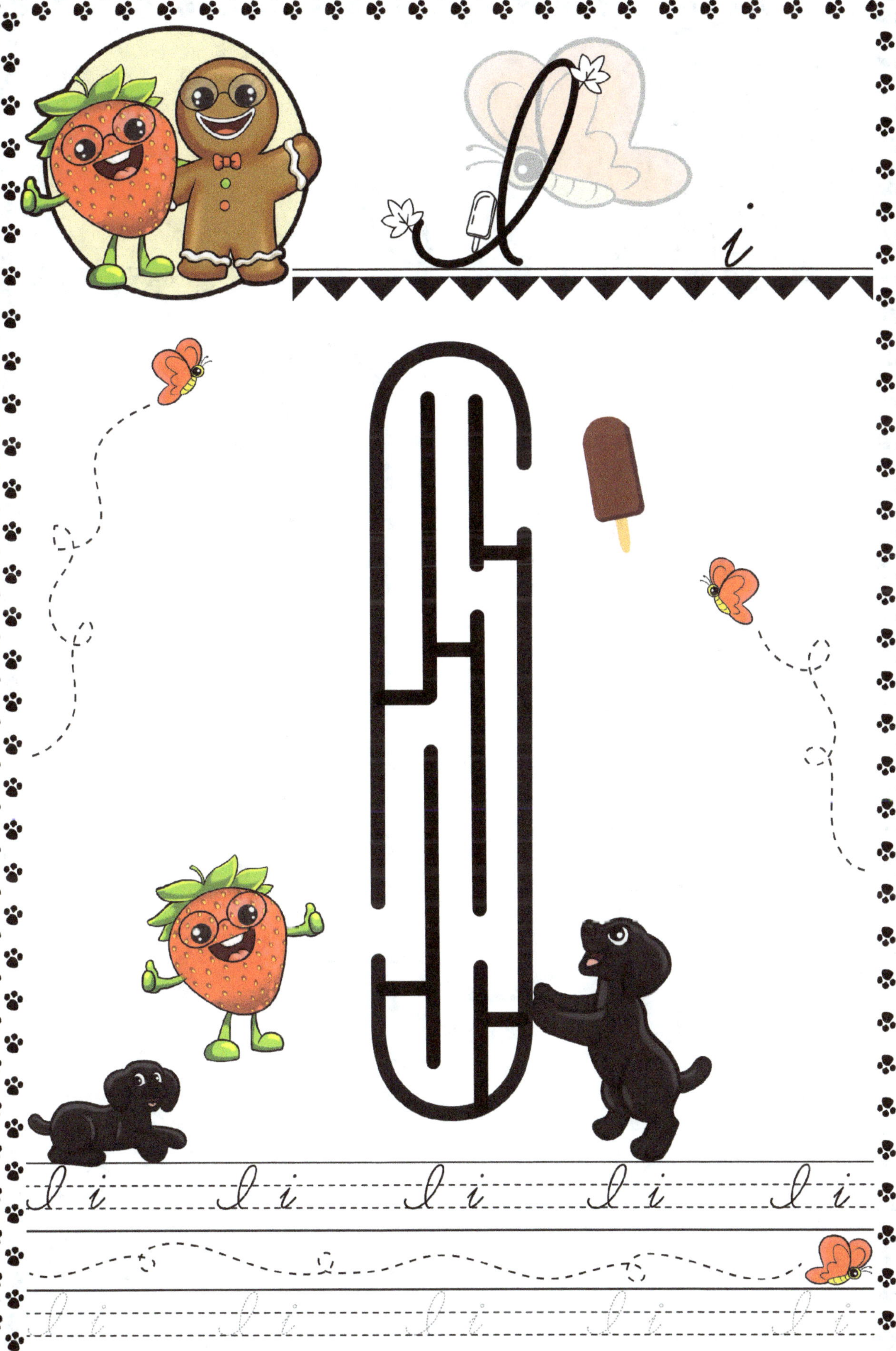

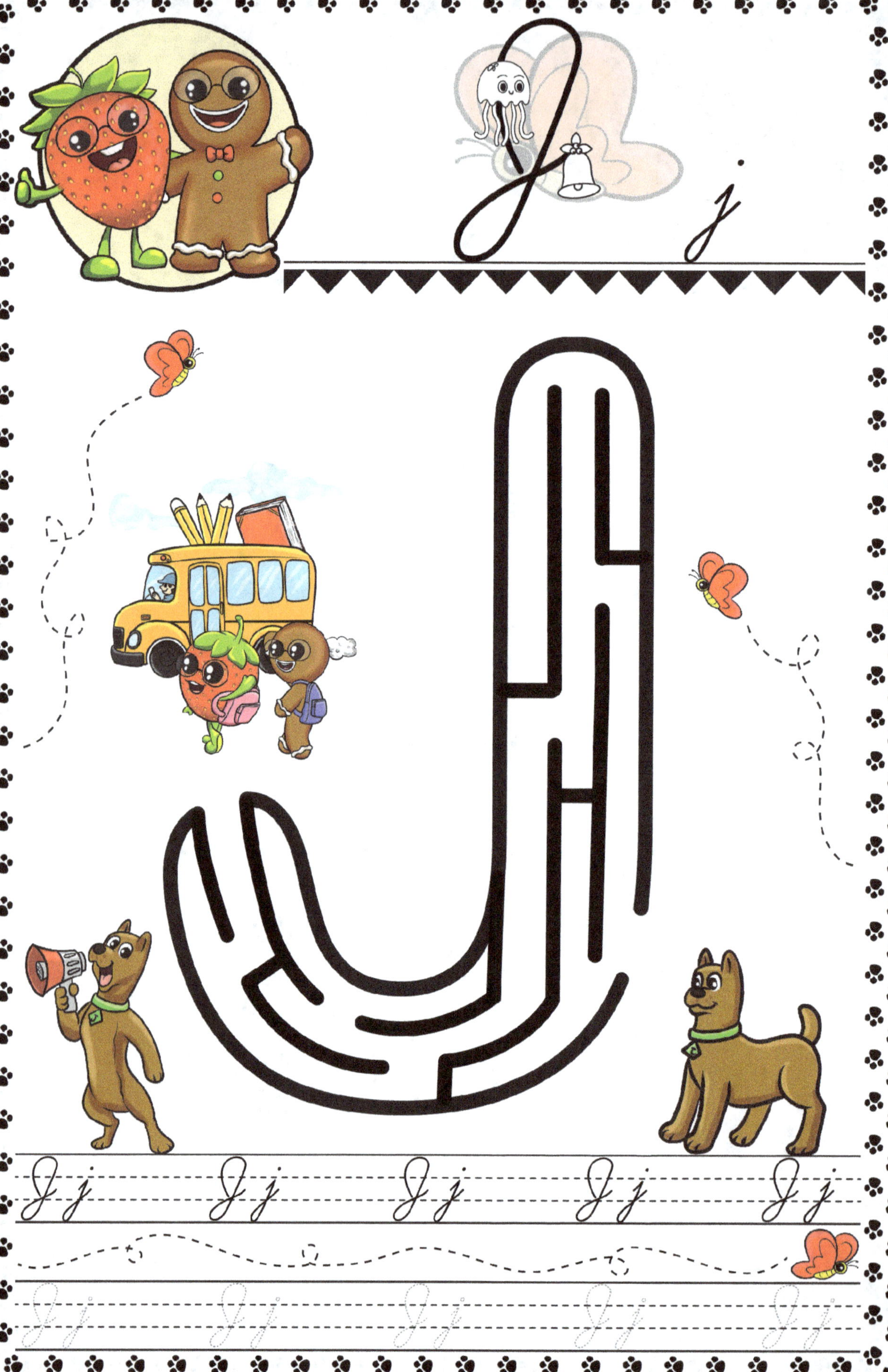

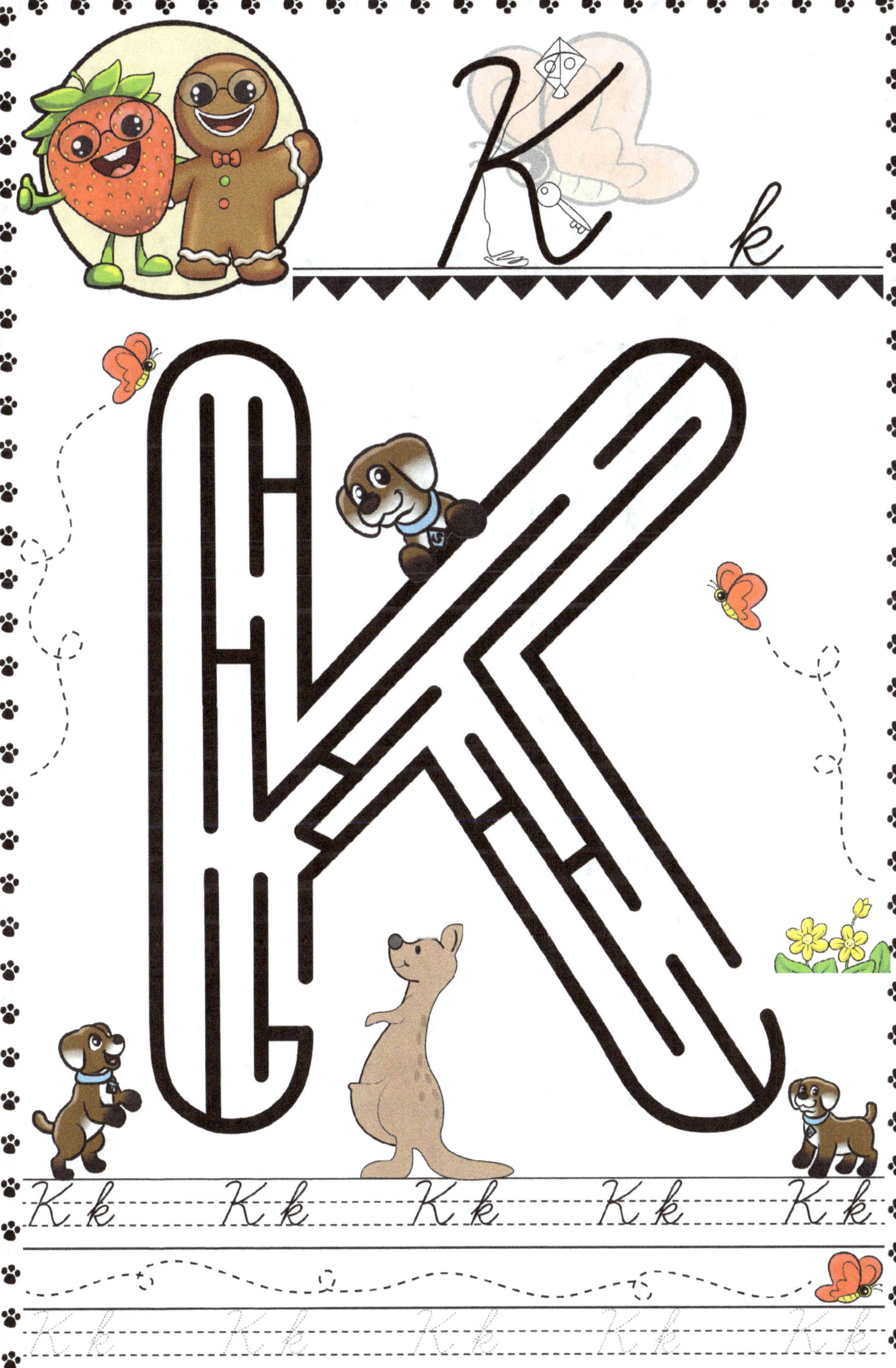
K
k
K k   K k   K k   K k   K k

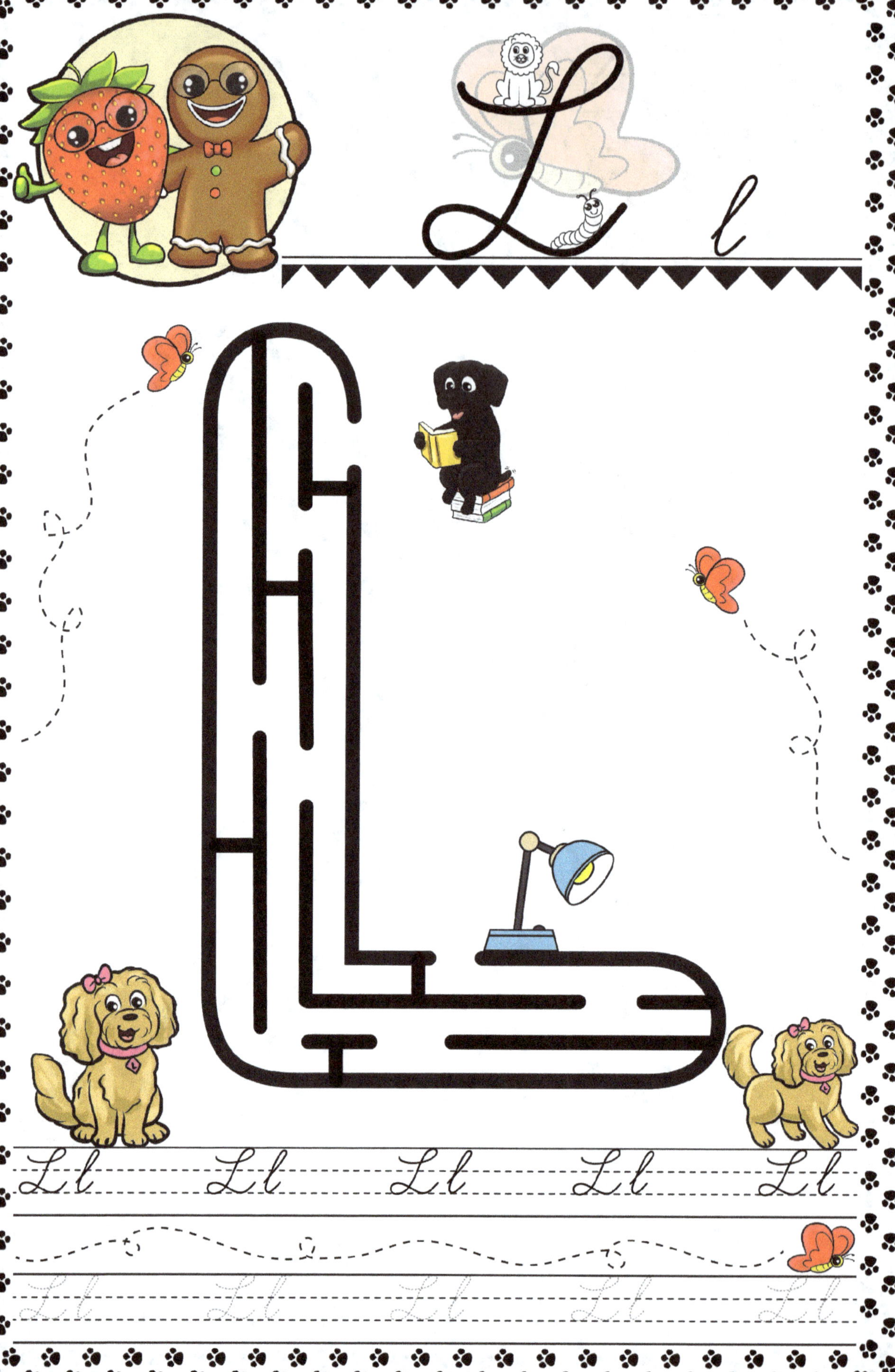

$\mathcal{L}$ ℓ

$\mathcal{L}\ell$ $\mathcal{L}\ell$ $\mathcal{L}\ell$ $\mathcal{L}\ell$ $\mathcal{L}\ell$

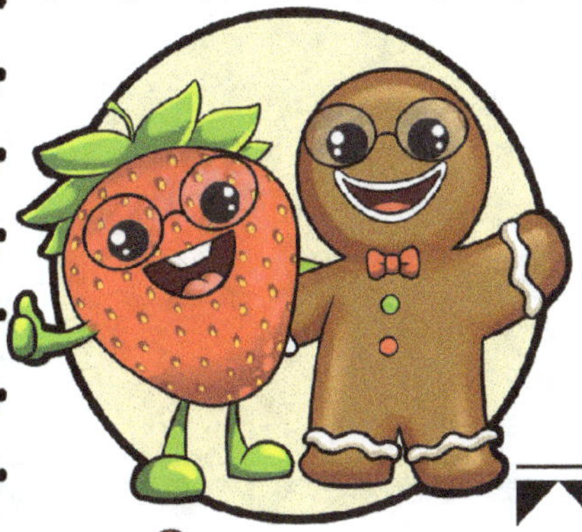

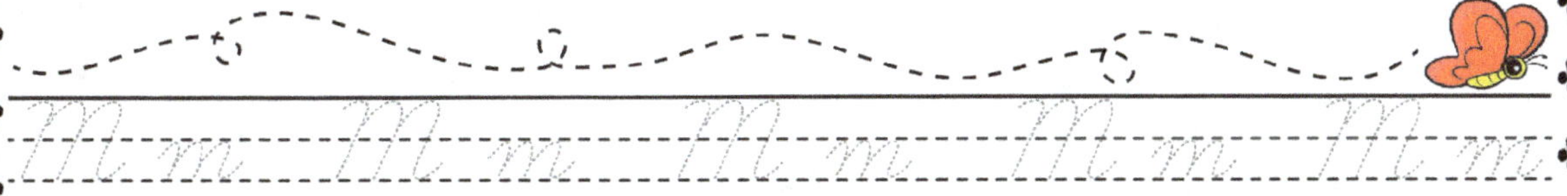

m m m m m m m m m m

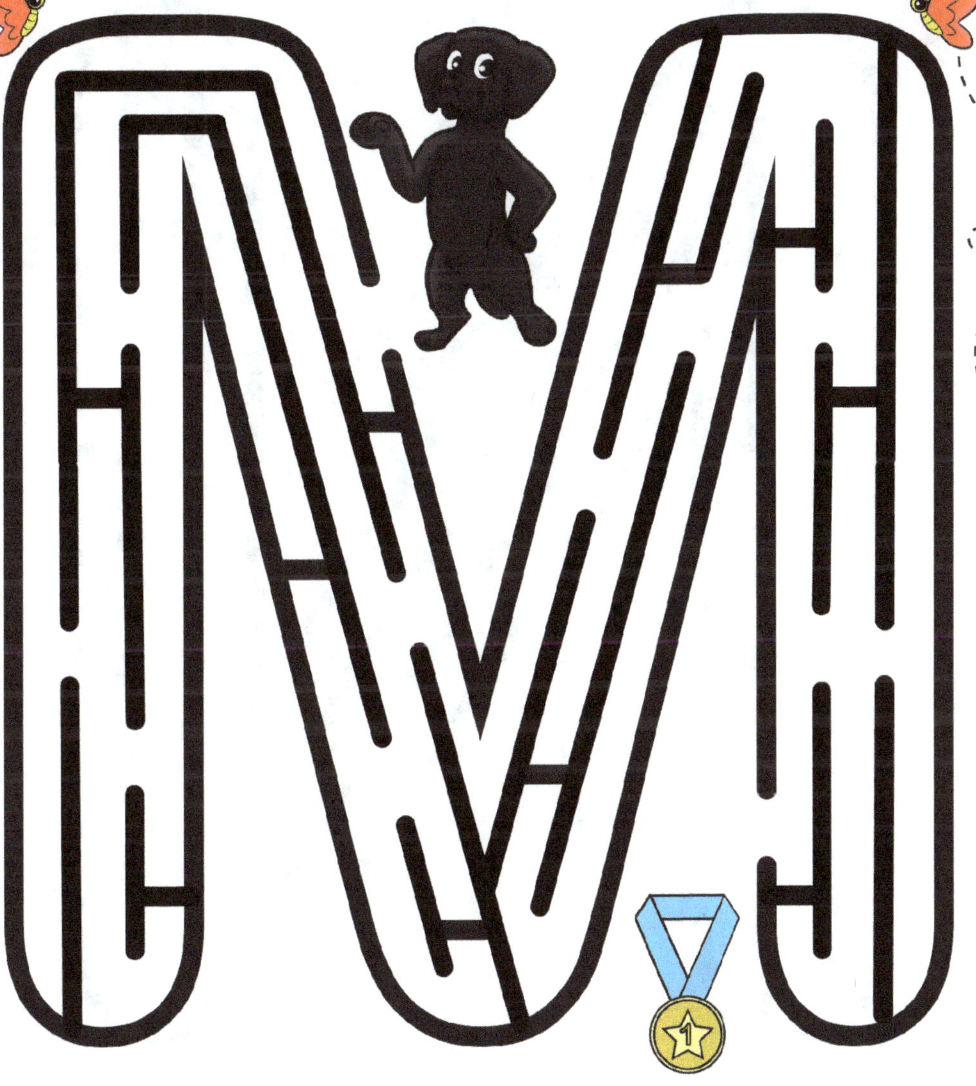

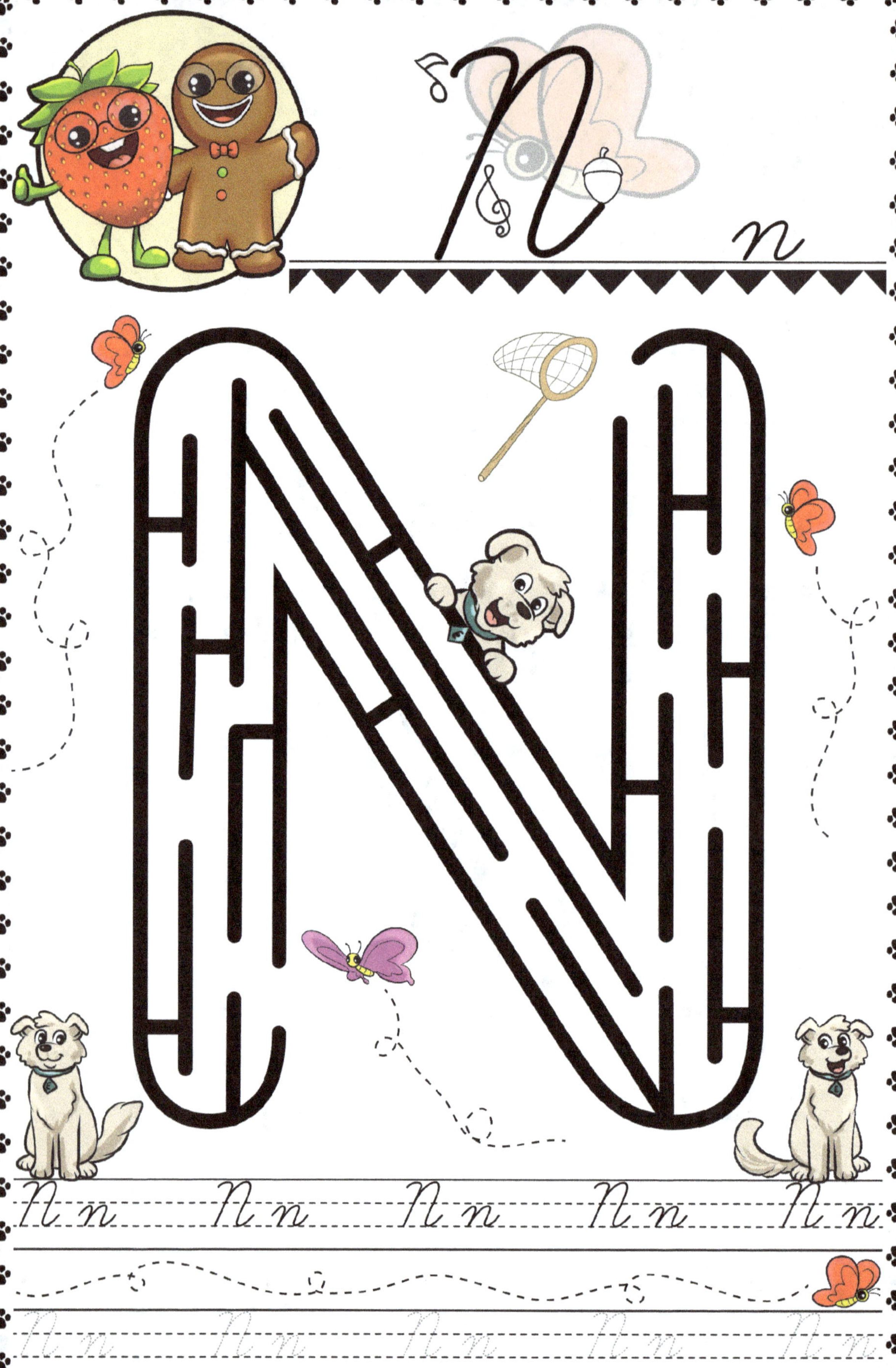

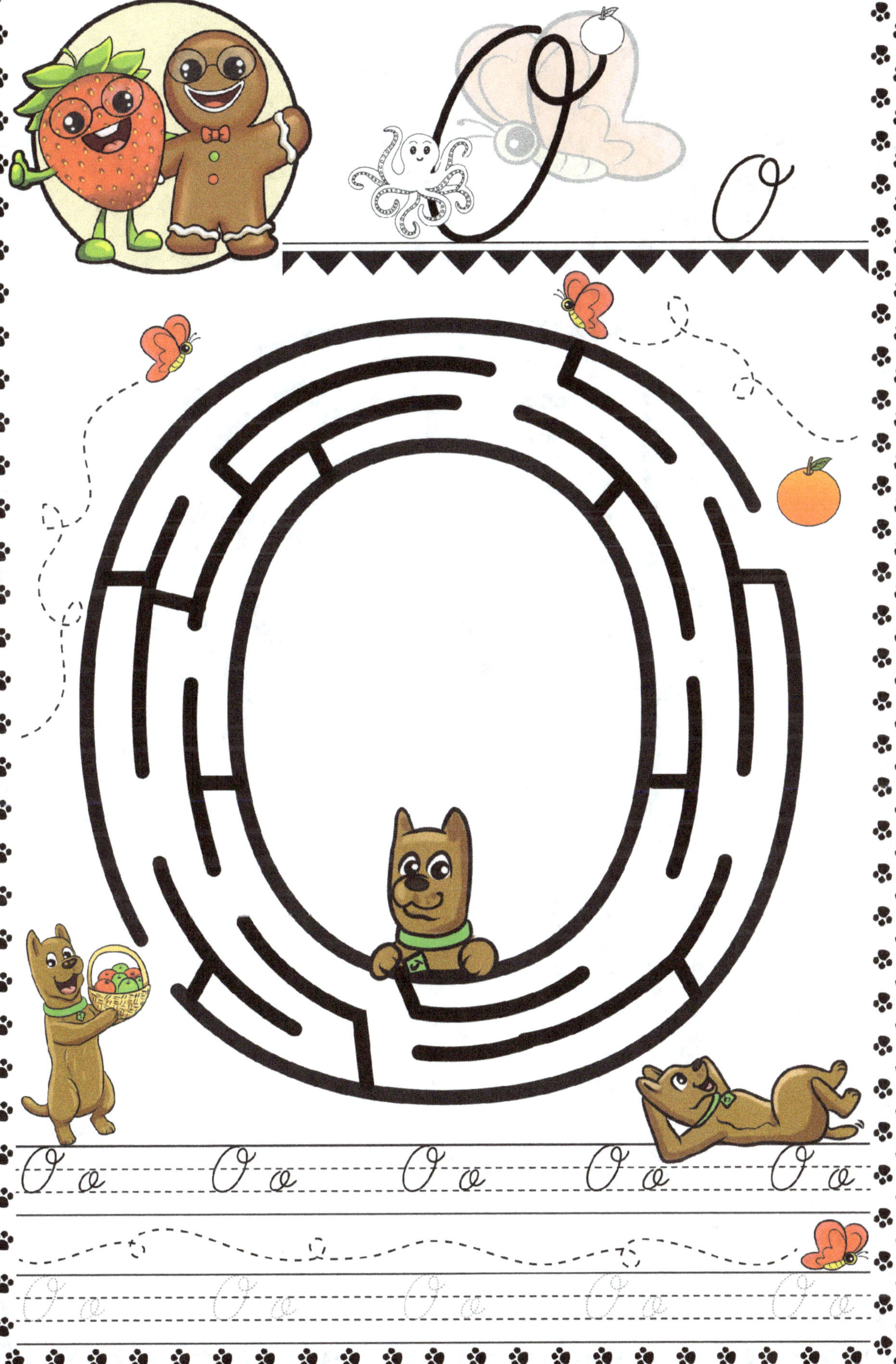

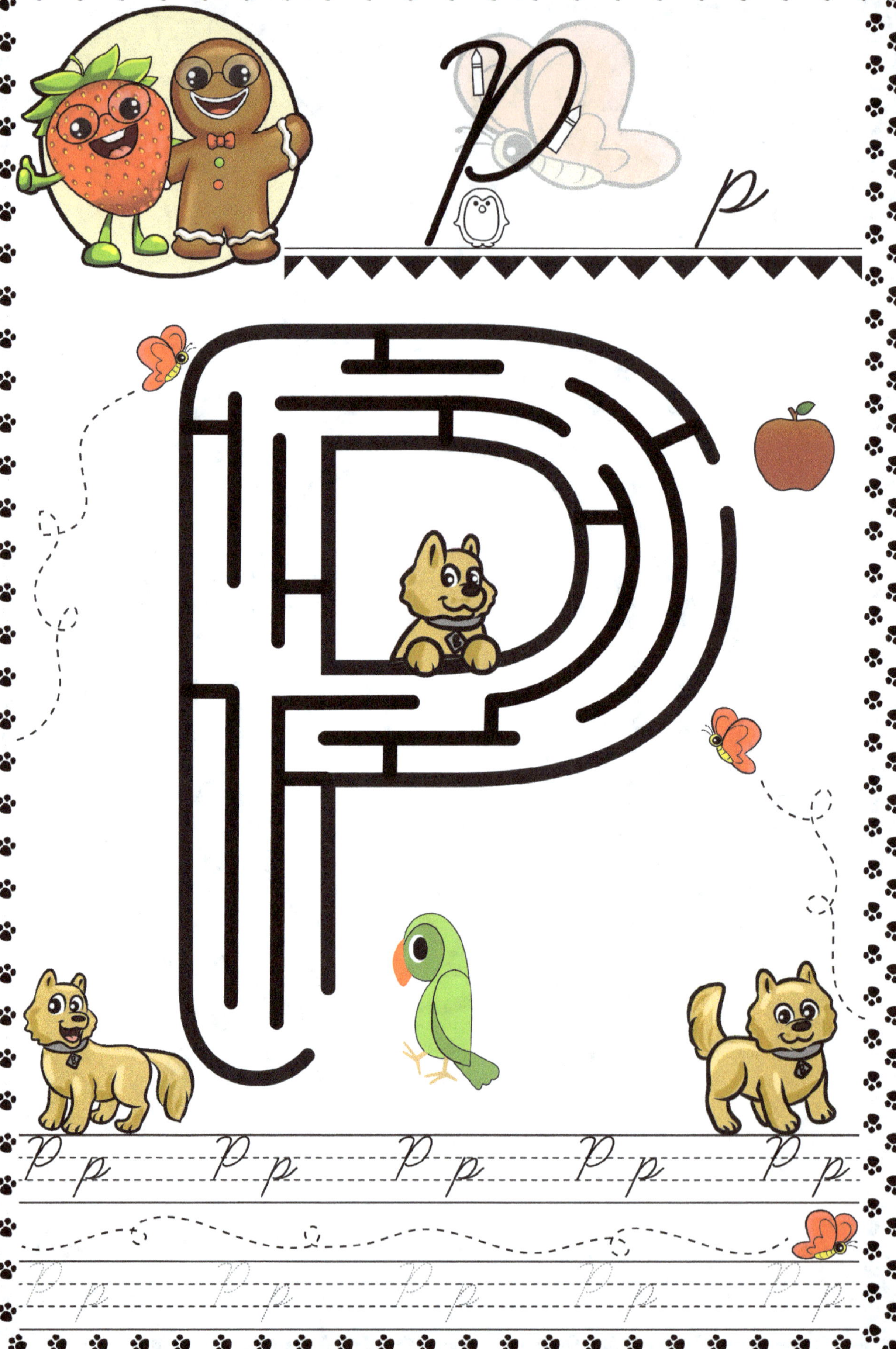

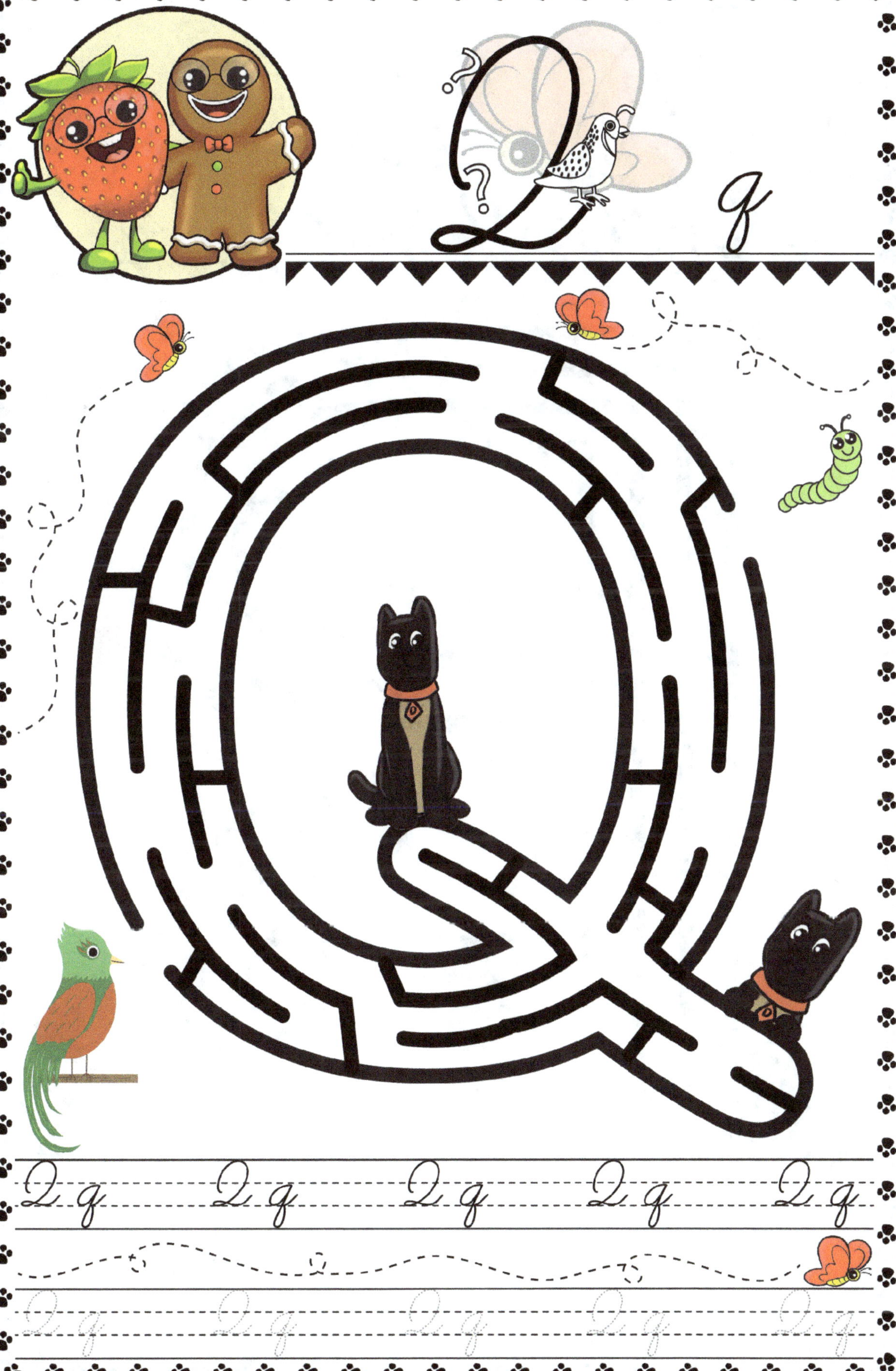

q

2q 2q 2q 2q 2q

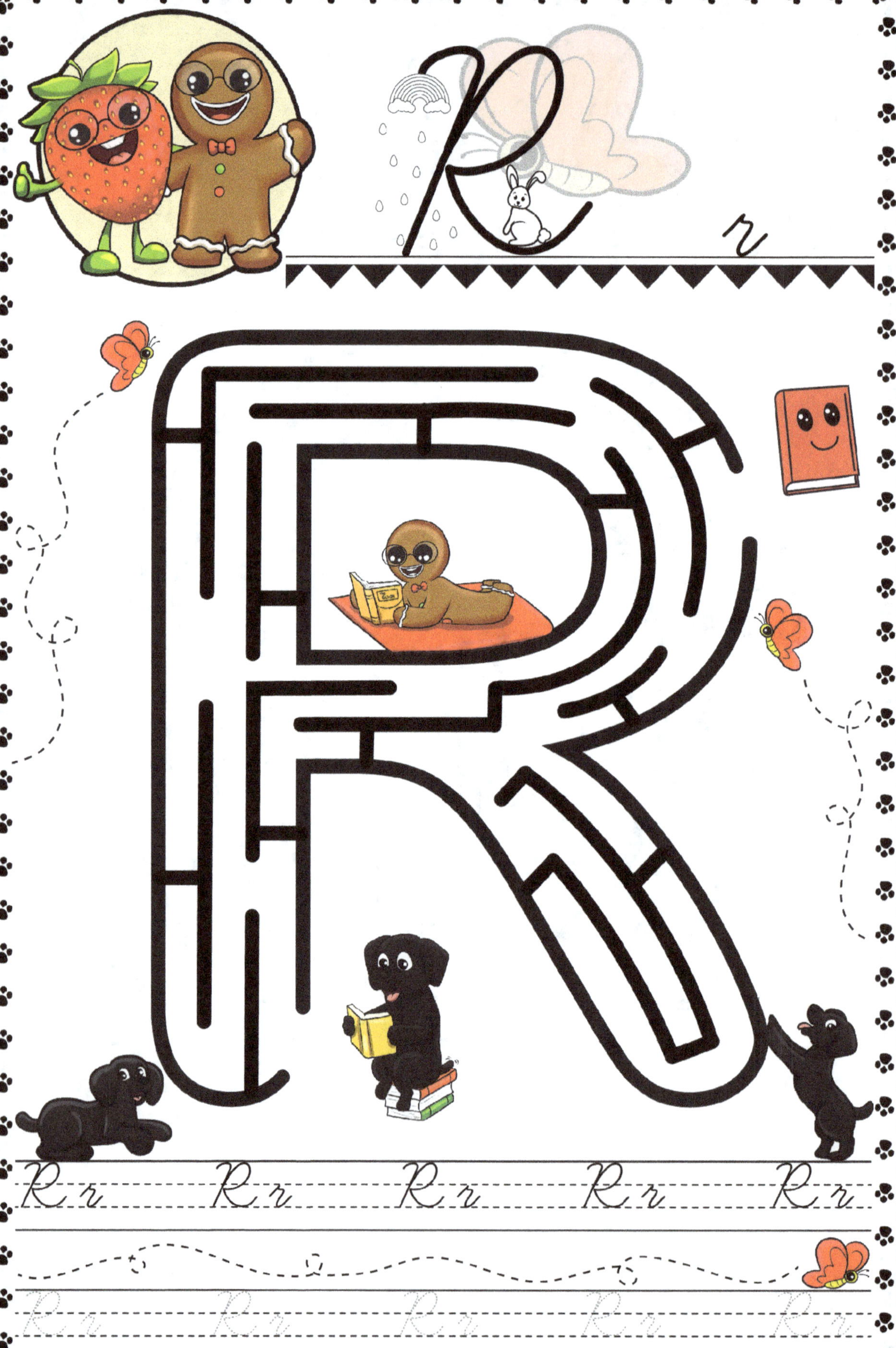

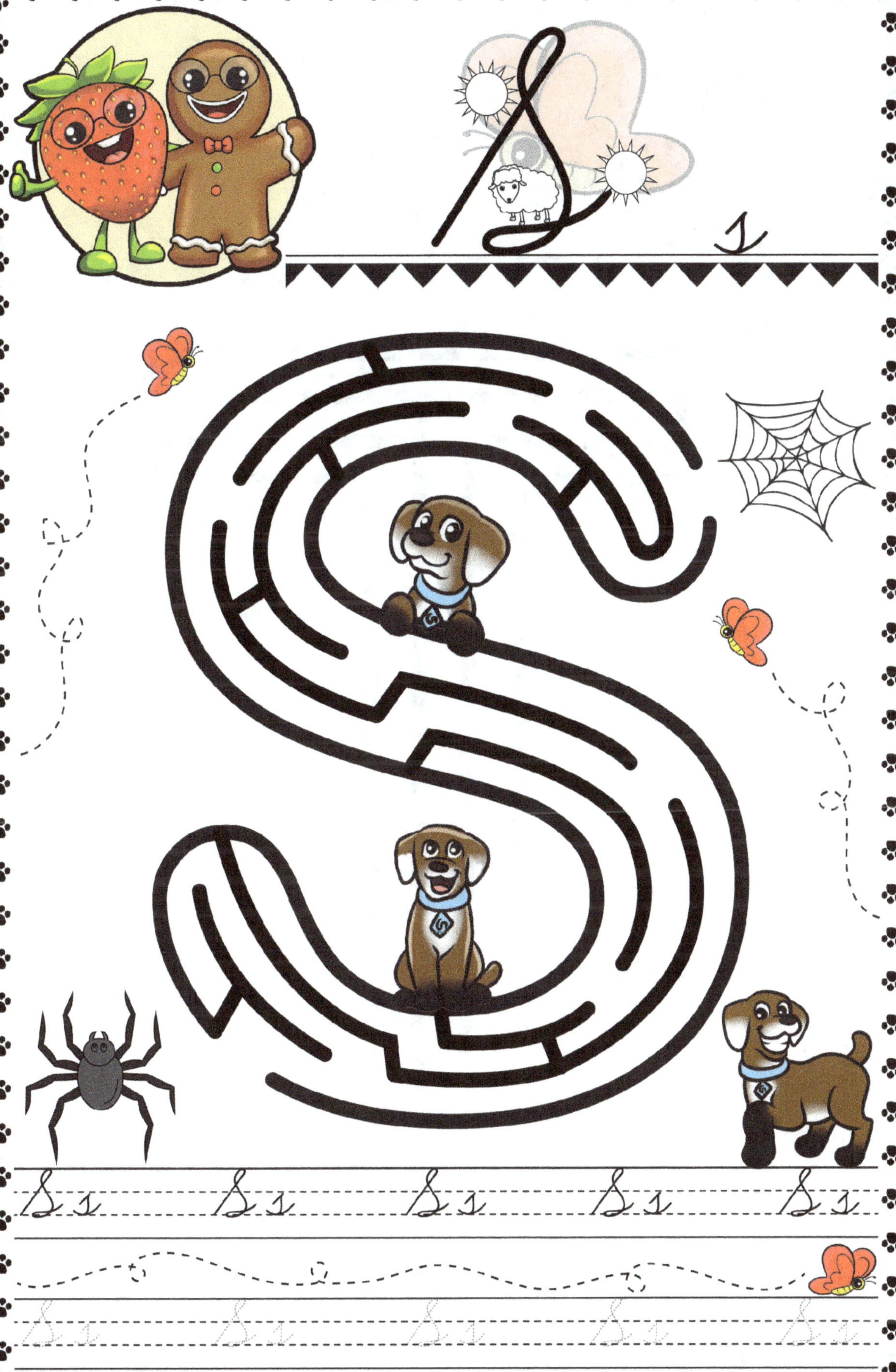

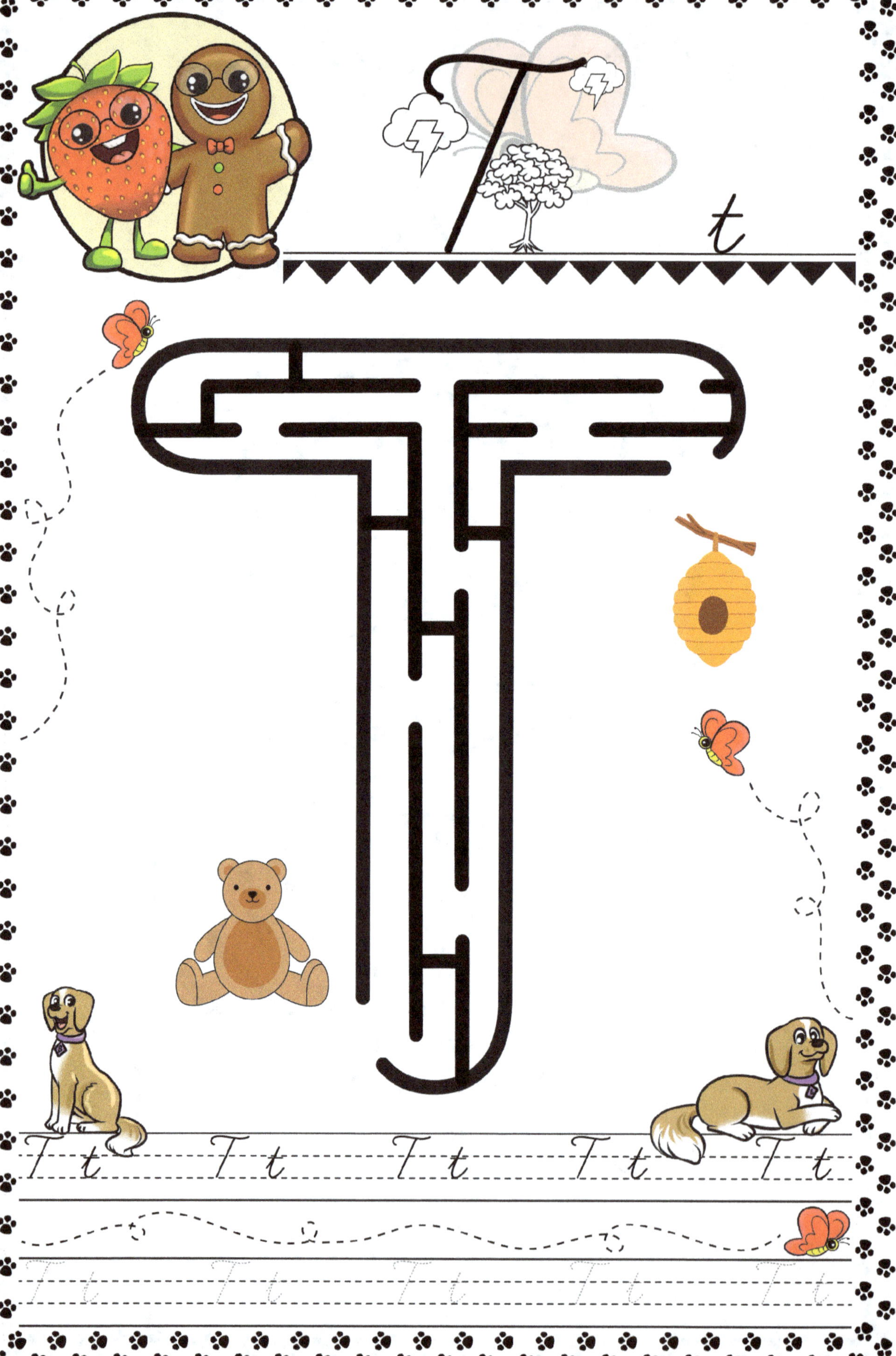

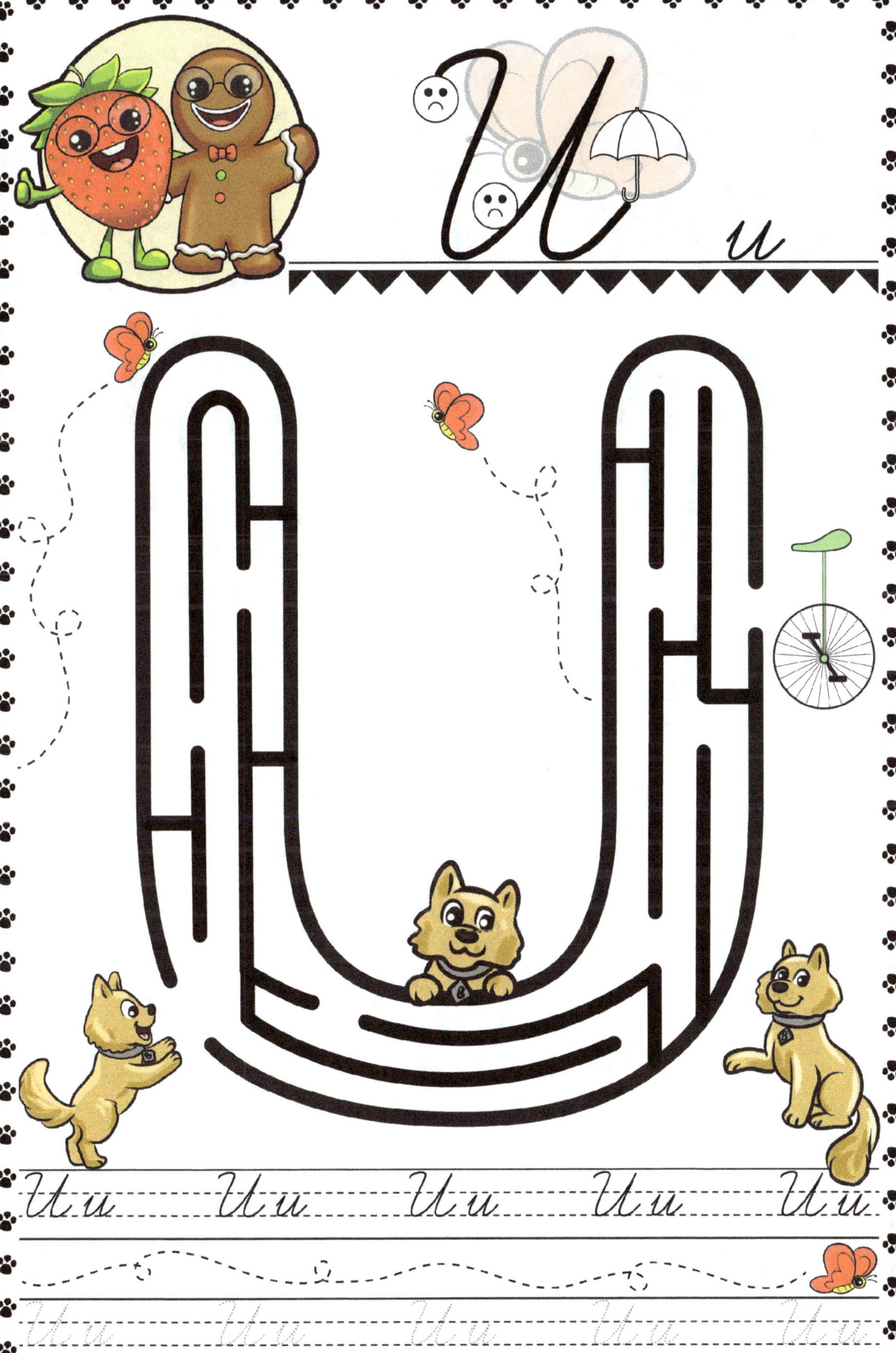
И
и
Ии Ии Ии Ии Ии
Ии Ии Ии Ии Ии

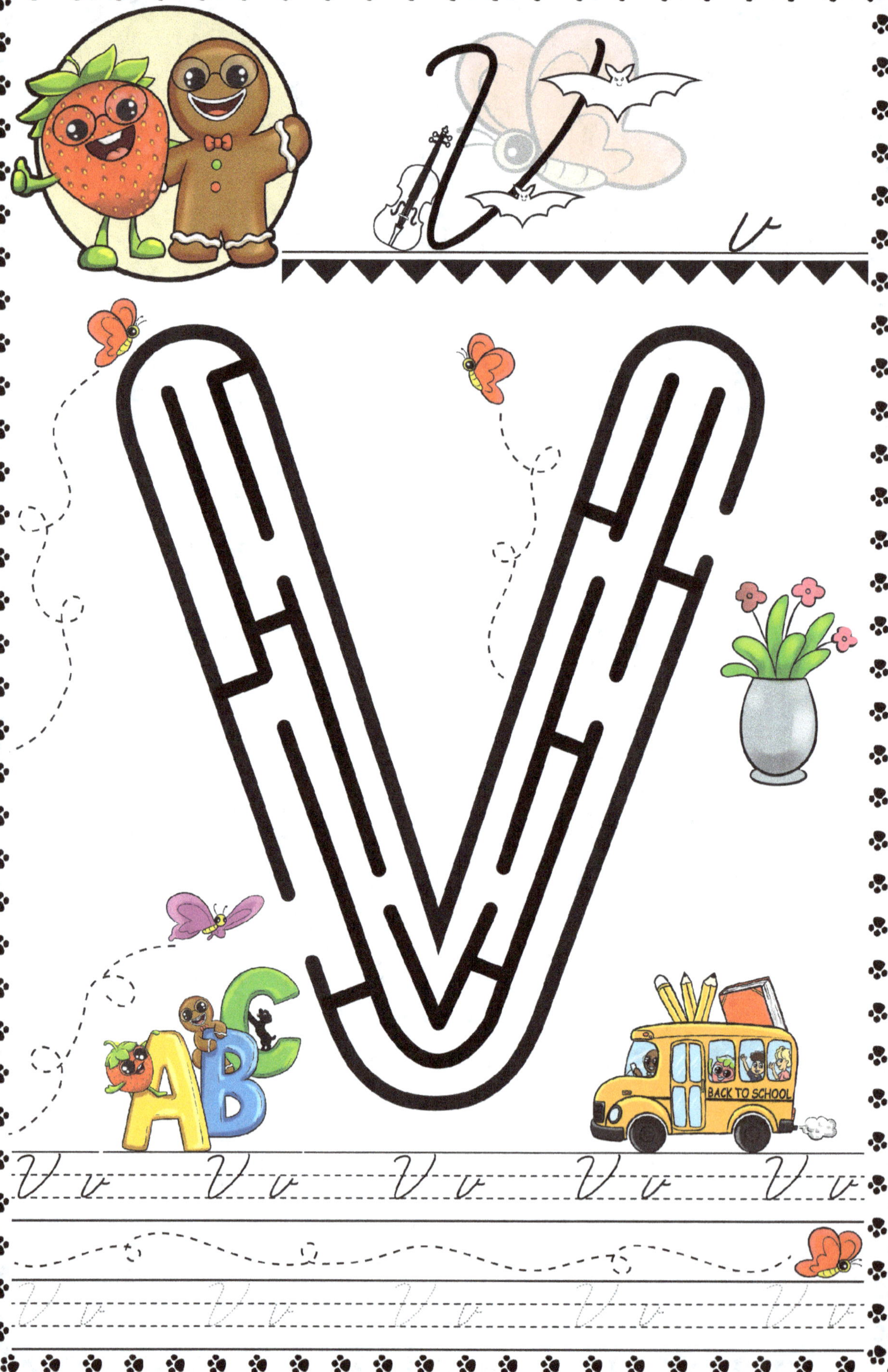

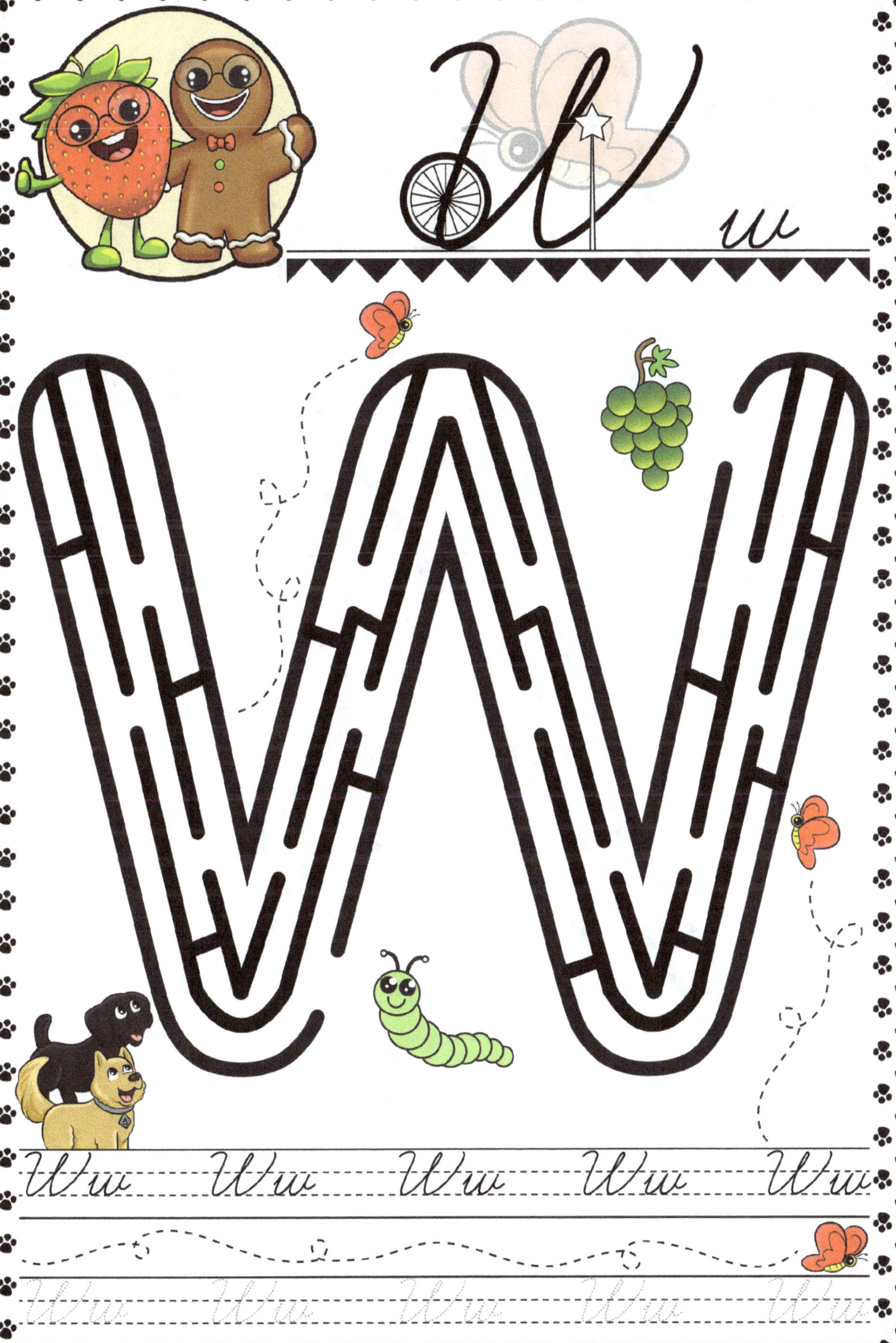

Ww   Ww   Ww   Ww   Ww

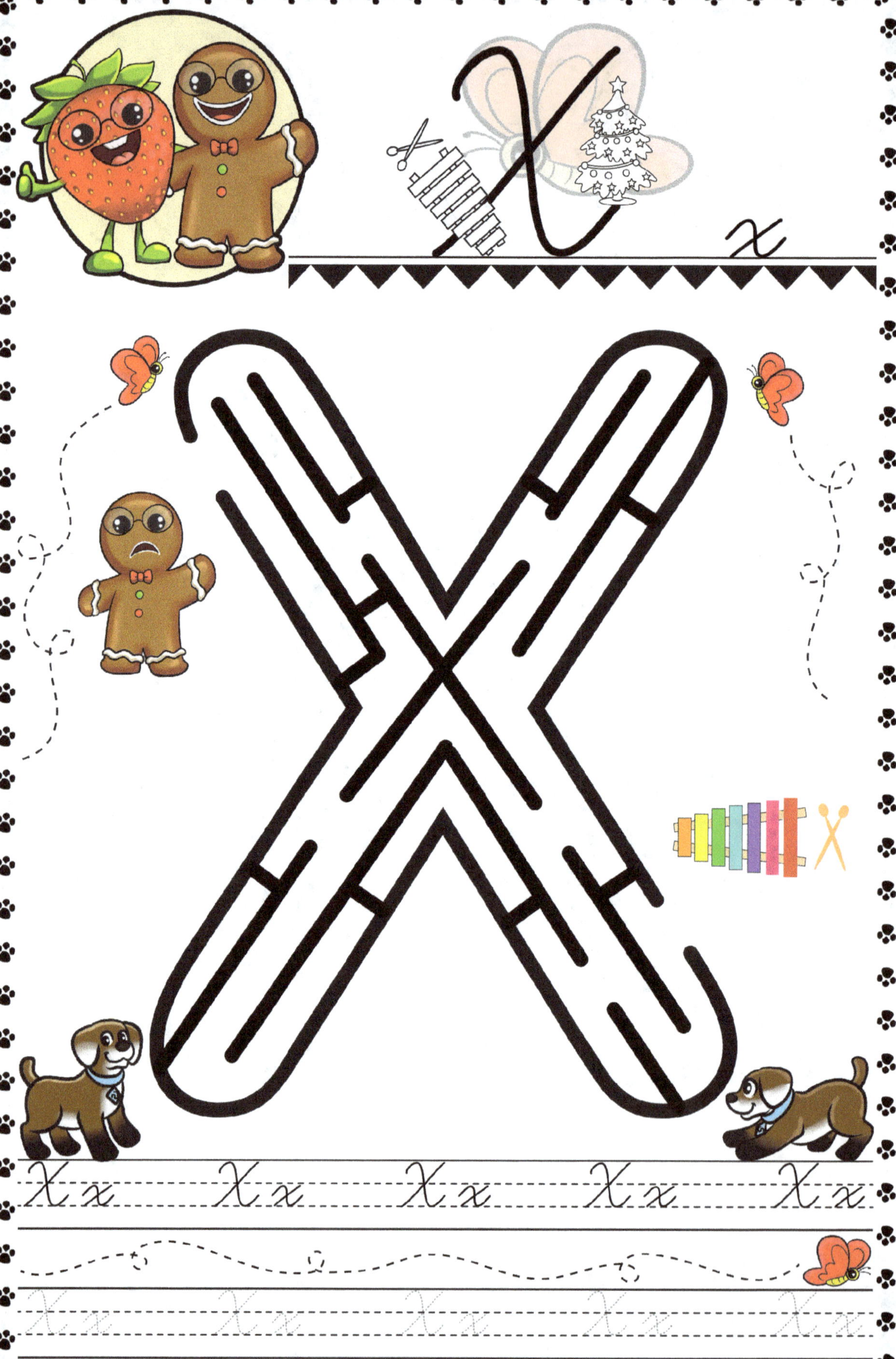

X x   X x   X x   X x   X x

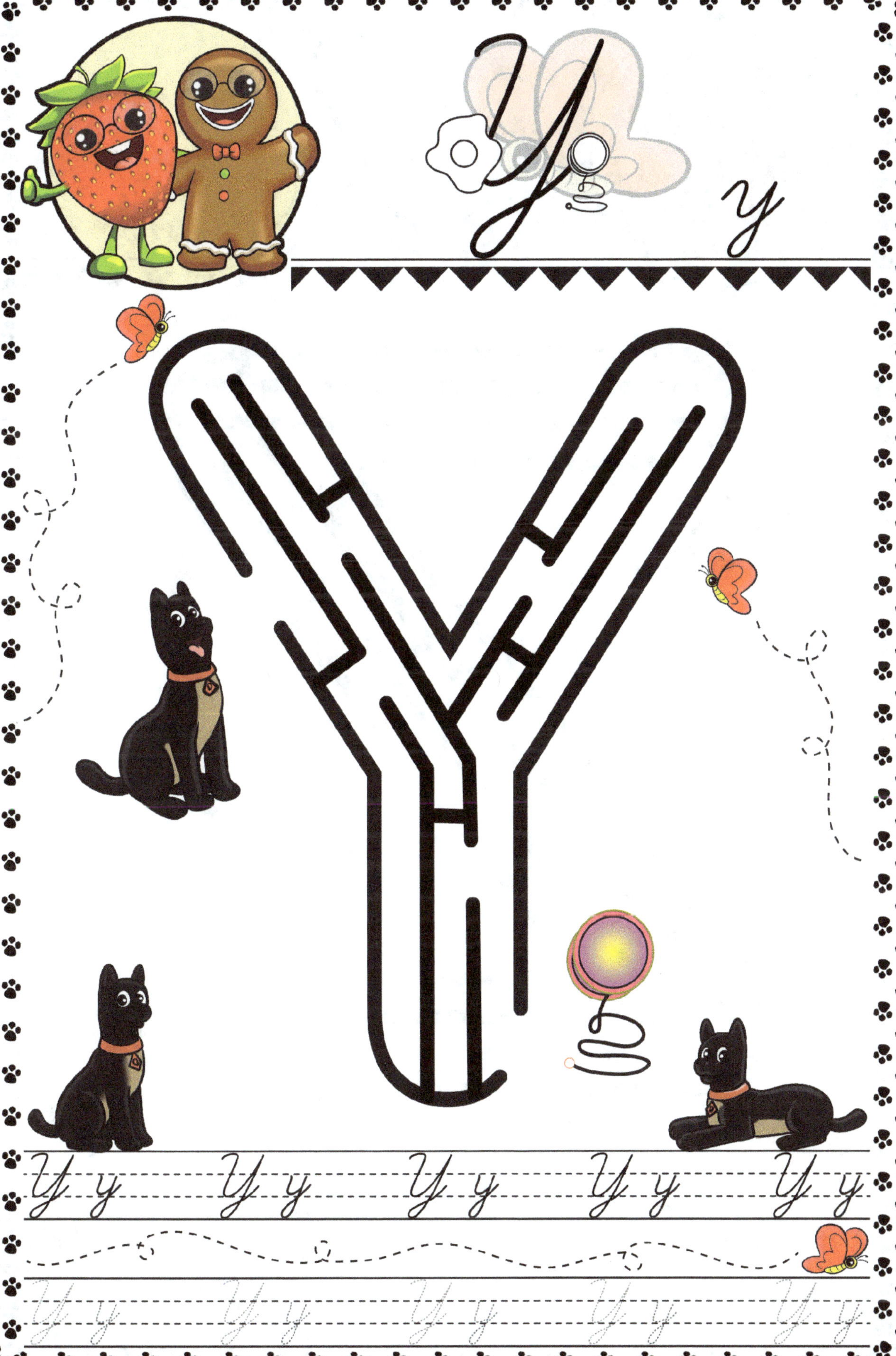

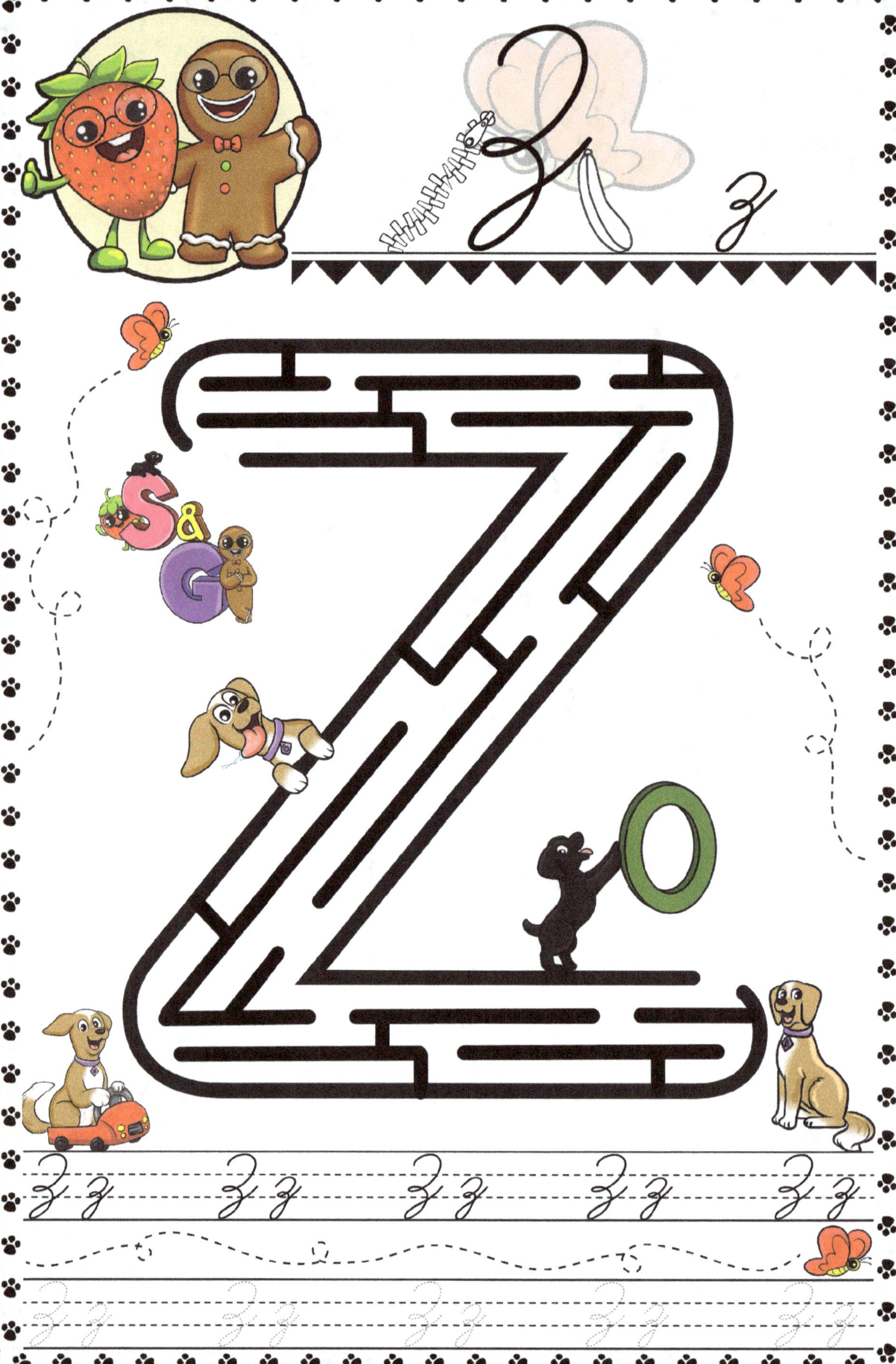

A	B	C	D	E
F	G	H	I	J
K	L	M	N	O
P	Q	R	S	T
U	V	W	X	Y
		Z		

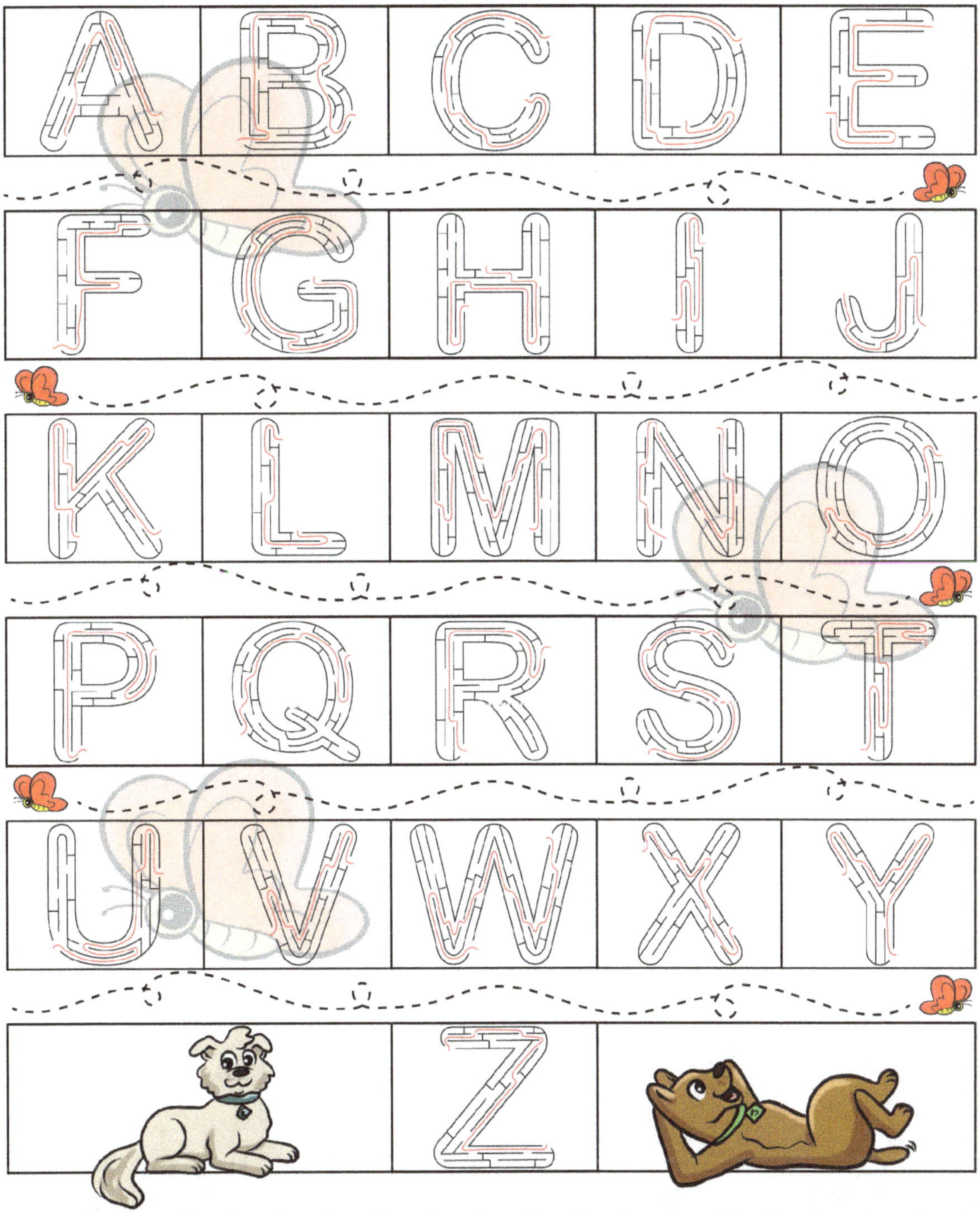

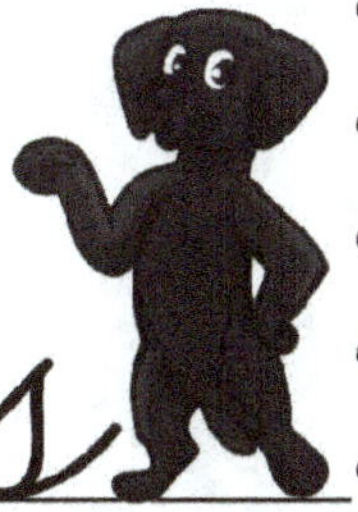